IMAGES OF ENGLAND

HORNSEY AND CROUCH END

HORNSEY.

FORTITOR QUO PARATIOR

THE CLOCK TOWER, CROUCH END.

IMAGES OF ENGLAND

HORNSEY AND CROUCH END

KEN GAY

The
History
Press

First published in 1998 by
The Chalford Publishing Company

Reprinted in 2008 by
The History Press
The Mill, Brimscombe Port,
Stroud, Gloucestershire, GL5 2QG
www.thehistorypress.co.uk

Reprinted 2011

ISBN 978 0 7524 1072 2

Printed and bound in England.

Contents

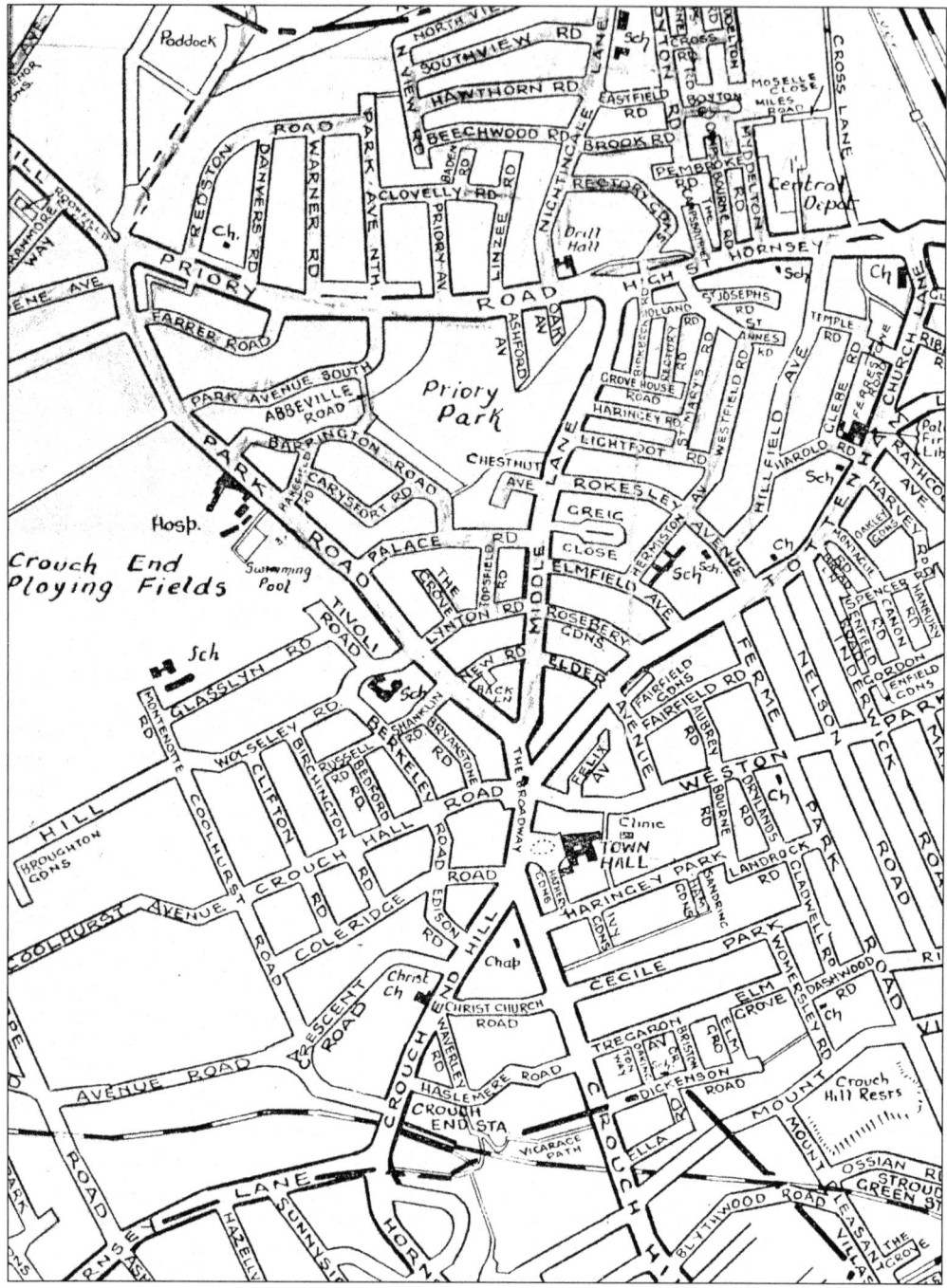

Map of the area, c. 1938.

Introduction

Hornsey and Crouch End are the place names of two former Middlesex villages. Both remained rural until the 1870s but they are now part of the northern, residential suburbs of London. These photographs attempt to capture the change.

Small and sparsely populated, the two villages were for a long time an attraction for middle-class Londoners seeking a place in the countryside within reach of their businesses. In the eighteenth and nineteenth centuries merchants and professionals who had done well in their careers bought older properties, or built new ones, in the undulating wooded area. Enjoying their rural acres they travelled by horse or coach the five miles to the Metropolis.

Among such men was Jacob Warner, a London grocer who in 1796 took over the Priory and was to rebuild it; William Eady, a goldsmith, who in 1853 moved into the old Hornsey estate of Campsbourne; William Bird, an ironmaster who in the 1850s took over Crouch Hall from the Booths, the distillers, who had built it in the place of Old Crouch Hall across the Broadway, Crouch End; Henry Weston Elder, a bristle merchant who bought Topsfield Hall and its estate lands in 1853; and up Crouch Hill in the area known as Mount Pleasant were villas similarly owned. Muswell Hill echoed the pattern, with Clays the printers, and William Block, silk merchant, in substantial estates on the hill leading from Hornsey.

Wooden and brick cottages and some shops made up the rest of the settlements, housing the craftsmen, tradesmen and others needed to maintain the houses and look after the pasture land which provided dairy products and grazing land for sheep or transitory cattle. The area was also a place for out-of-town schools, the most famous being the Crouch End Academy, established in the seventeenth century and lasting till the end of the nineteenth, whose boy boarders must have brought a youthful vibrancy to the quiet hamlet. Leisure pursuits was another role, with Londoners seeking out local country pubs on public holidays, perhaps to fish in the New River. By 1863 Alexandra Park had opened and its race track of 1868 was soon attracting punters along Park Road from London, to be offered from 1873 visits to the huge bulk of Alexandra Palace, which loomed over Hornsey village.

Both villages (along with Muswell Hill, Stroud Green and part of Highgate) were in the parish of Hornsey, with the Bishop of London, lord of the manor of Hornsey, appointing the rector. Hornsey, Haringey, Harringay and other variant spellings of the local place name derive from Old English and are taken to mean 'the enclosure of Haering or of Haering's people'. So it is logical to conclude that, despite Roman coins found in the area, Hornsey village first grew as an Anglo-Saxon settlement in the Forest of Middlesex. It was probably the oldest settlement as it gave its name to the parish. At the centre of Hornsey village was the parish church, first recorded in the thirteenth century.

Crouch End lay to the south of Hornsey village at the junction of crossroads, and it is likely that a cross stood here, giving the settlement its name (meaning Cross End), first recorded in 1465. As Peter Barber has argued in his illuminating research into Crouch End in *People and Places - Lost Estates in Highgate, Hornsey and Wood Green*, the cross would have marked the boundary of the two largest local estates: Rowledge Farm belonging to the Bishop of London on the west and Topsfield estate on the east, which by 1374 'had gained a considerable degree of autonomy from the manor of Hornsey and had evolved into the sub-manor of Topsfield or Broadgate'.

Hornsey and Crouch End have changed with the growth of London as a world capital based on trade, finance and manufacturing talents such as those of the clockmakers of Clerkenwell or the shipbuilders on the Thames. London's population expanded from about one million at the beginning of the nineteenth century to about four million at the end. The new population needed homes to live in. The development of mechanical forms of transport, primarily the steam train, later the bicycle and the tram - comparatively cheap forms of travel - led to London's hinterland being rapidly transformed.

Change for Hornsey began with the arrival in 1850 of the Great Northern Railway's main line to the north from London, with Hornsey as its first stop, the first of several railways locally. In the late 1860s Campsbourne and Grove House estates in Hornsey village began to be built over and as landowners sold their properties the equivalent of a new town was built over the green spaces. Hornsey became a borough in 1903. Its parish population had increased from 11,082 in 1861 to 72,056 by 1901. Its 1951 peak was 98,159. Crouch End became an important local shopping centre and in 1935 was chosen as the site for a new town hall.

These photographs include some early ones before urbanization. Edwardian pictures capture people in their High Street or show the terraced roads and new buildings that changed the landscape. It is hoped that they will help residents in their understanding of the place in which they live.

Acknowledgements

The majority of the images come from the archive of the Hornsey Historical Society. I am indebted to the society for permission to reproduce them in this book. Some of the other views are from my own collection but more come from the collection of Dick Whetstone and Hugh Garnsworthy who have both generously loaned material. Mrs Hilda Wright has kindly loaned the photo of the British Legion dinner on page 123. Peter Garland has kindly provided the drawing on page 25. I thank everybody for their co-operation, without which this book would not have been possible. The text is my own.

For those seeking to know more about Hornsey and Crouch End and adjacent places such as Highgate, Muswell Hill, Stroud Green and Wood Green, the Hornsey Historical Society is able to help. Over the past three decades it has issued historical maps, postcards and books covering the area. Membership offers talks, visits and social occasions; details from 136 Tottenham Lane, London, N8 7EL.

Ken Gay

One

Hornsey Church
and Rectory

St Mary's was the parish church for an area which for centuries remained rural and under-populated, as indicated by this 1771 view. The Middlesex countryside was to change as London expanded.

Hornsey church is first recorded in 1291 when English churches were listed for papal taxation. Its date of origin is unknown but Hornsey is an Old English place name and this might have been a site for worship in Saxon times. Registers of baptisms, marriages and deaths date from 1654.

Hornsey — The Old Church

Hornsey church photographed in Edwardian times. The nave of white brick dates from 1832 when the medieval structure was replaced by this one designed by architect George Smith. The tower was retained for bell-ringing but heightened; it dates from at least 1500.

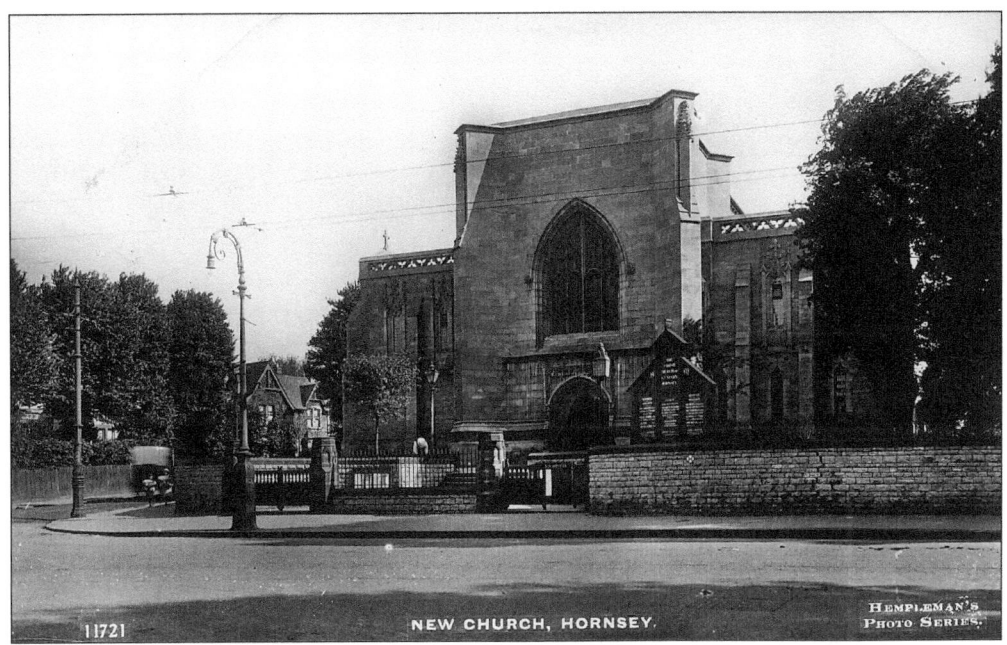

The New church was built in 1889 to replace the one rebuilt in 1832 which proved too small as the local population expanded. Non-orientated and built in the angle between Church Lane and Hornsey High Street (where St Mary's Infants' School now stands), it was designed by architect James Brooks and seated 1,200, with a Willis organ installed. It survived until 1969.

Old and New church stood side by side from 1889 until 1927 when the old church nave was demolished, leaving only the tower, still used for bell-ringing. The New church developed cracks and was demolished under the St Mary (Hornsey) Act 1969. Services were held in the National Hall in the High Street until the congregation joined with St George's in Cranley Gardens to form the church of St Mary with St George, where some of the memorials from the previous church were installed.

Hornsey gravedigger David Dye, with clay pipe, in a studio portrait probably of the 1860s. Use of the graveyard for burials ended by an 1872 Order in Council in December 1877, except in existing vaults and graves. For centuries before, local people had been buried in Hornsey churchyard. As the population expanded new burial places had to be established.

Chest tombs and gravestones are still to be seen in Hornsey churchyard long after Mr Dye's work had finished. A chest tomb near the High Street is that of Samuel Rogers (1763-1855), the banker-poet who declined the poet laureateship on the death in 1850 of William Wordsworth. Charles Dickens, whose sister lived nearby, mentions Hornsey churchyard in *David Copperfield* as the burial place of Betsy Trotswood's husband.

Old Hornsey Church.

The medieval church tower is the oldest remaining building in Hornsey. In 1950 the site of the nave was dedicated as a Garden of Remembrance and is used each November as the place for a civic service attended by the British Legion. Wreaths of poppies are laid at the foot of the tower. A charity named Friends of Hornsey Church Tower was formed in 1989 and has restored the tower so that it can be ascended to the top on open days organized by the charity. The Friends are working with the Parochial Church Council, Haringey Borough Council, the adjacent St Mary's Infants' School and others to improve the tower and churchyard still further, and to ensure it is kept in good condition.

Richard Harvey was Rector of Hornsey from 1829 to 1881 and saw the parish change from a rural to an urban one. A tall, aristrocratic man, he was an effective rector who created six new districts and churches in the parish to meet the needs of a population which rose from under 6,000 in 1841 to over 37,000 in 1881. (It was to rise to 61,000 in 1891, and to a peak in 1951 of over 98,000.)

A rectory house existed by 1320 with the living in the gift of the Bishop of London, lord of the manor of Hornsey. A rectory estate of 1½acres was at the western end of Hornsey High Street (see map on page 20). The rectory house was rebuilt in 1851 and extended in 1890 but demolished in the 1960s when the site was mostly used for a church school. A replacement rectory existed there from 1964 to 1989.

'HORNSEY RECTORY 1832'

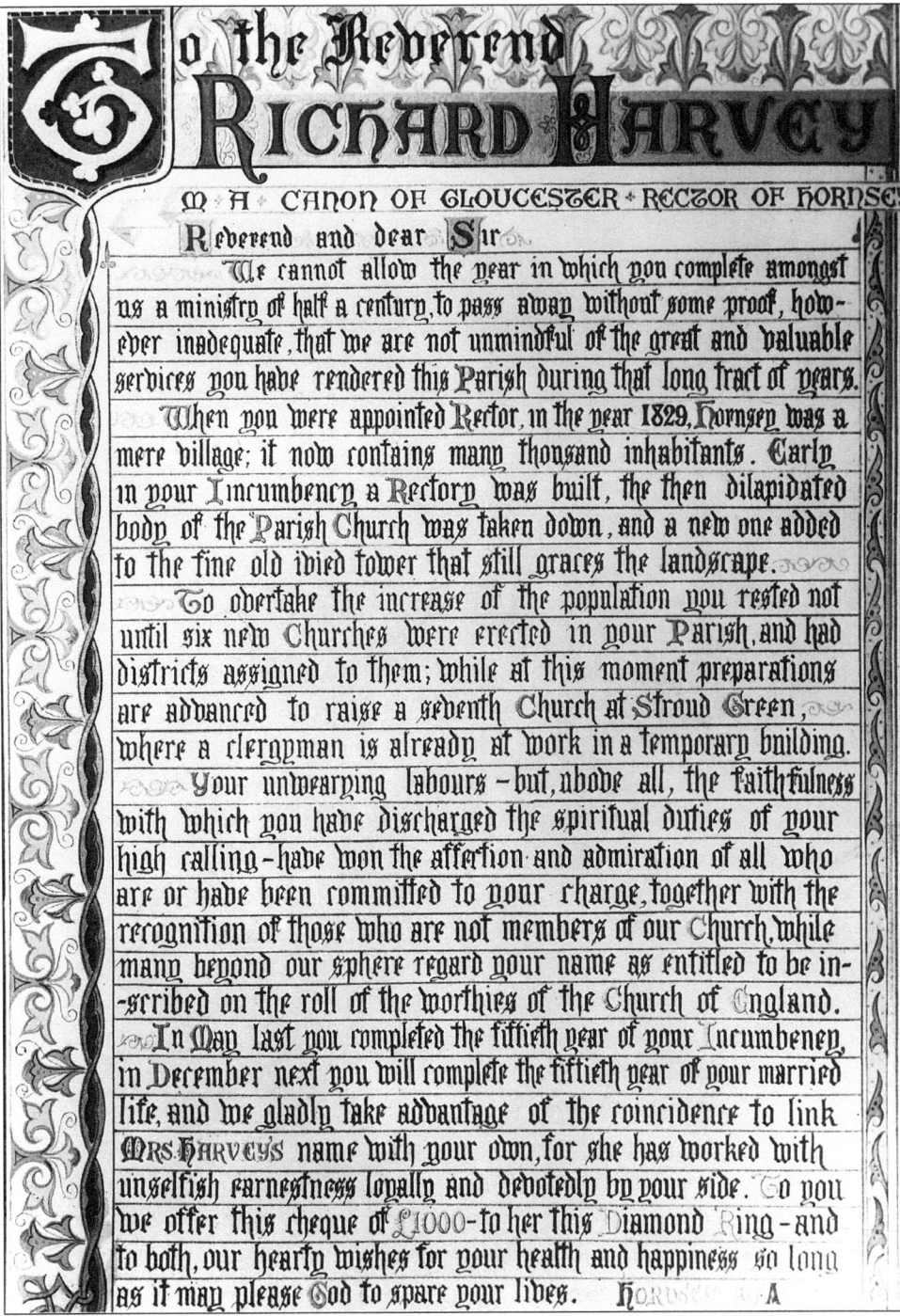

To the Reverend RICHARD HARVEY

M · A · CANON OF GLOUCESTER · RECTOR OF HORNSEY

Reverend and dear Sir

We cannot allow the year in which you complete amongst us a ministry of half a century, to pass away without some proof, however inadequate, that we are not unmindful of the great and valuable services you have rendered this Parish during that long tract of years.

When you were appointed Rector, in the year 1829, Hornsey was a mere village; it now contains many thousand inhabitants. Early in your Incumbency a Rectory was built, the then dilapidated body of the Parish Church was taken down, and a new one added to the fine old ivied tower that still graces the landscape.

To obertake the increase of the population you rested not until six new Churches were erected in your Parish, and had districts assigned to them; while at this moment preparations are advanced to raise a seventh Church at Stroud Green, where a clergyman is already at work in a temporary building.

Your unwearying labours – but, above all, the faithfulness with which you have discharged the spiritual duties of your high calling – have won the affection and admiration of all who are or have been committed to your charge, together with the recognition of those who are not members of our Church, while many beyond our sphere regard your name as entitled to be inscribed on the roll of the worthies of the Church of England.

In May last you completed the fiftieth year of your Incumbency, in December next you will complete the fiftieth year of your married life, and we gladly take advantage of the coincidence to link Mrs Harvey's name with your own, for she has worked with unselfish earnestness loyally and devotedly by your side. To you we offer this cheque of £1000 – to her this Diamond Ring – and to both, our hearty wishes for your health and happiness so long as it may please God to spare your lives.

Testimonial volume to Richard Harvey to celebrate his 50 years' service as rector, presented to him in 1879. The large leather and brass bound book was ornamented with the Harvey crest and subscribed to by the parishioners. On retirement Harvey became Canon Residential at Gloucester; he and his wife died within 12 hours of each other in 1889 after 59 years of marriage.

Hornsey Rectory in the background with, grouped in front of it, ladies from the workhouse on an outing to Hornsey. Who the people at the rectory window are is not recorded. The tall top hat was fashionable in the 1860s, when this early photograph was probably taken.

Glebe Road, Hornsey. N.

Glebe Road takes its name from the land assigned to the parish incumbent as part of his benefice. The Rector of Hornsey had 48 acres of glebe land south of the parish church but refused to allow it to be developed for housing when Hornsey began to be urbanized in the late 1860s. By 1896 the glebe was only partly built up. Glebe Road was one of the roads.

Church Lane, Hornsey

Church Lane runs on the east side of the glebe land from Tottenham Lane to Hornsey High Street. In 1891 it contained only a row of eight houses on its west side. On the east side (right) were Ferrestone Lodge, Sunny Bank and Gisburne, three separate estates, though Ribblesdale Road had been partly built up.

Workhouse ladies on a visit to the rectory, but in this photograph the dark outdoor shawls and capes have been discarded and tea is about to be provided on the lawn. A workhouse stood in Hornsey High Street from 1735 but was demolished after poor law unions were formed under 1834 legislation. From that time Hornsey was joined with several other local parishes into the Edmonton Poor Law Union. From 1842 it had the workhouse near Silver Street, Edmonton, now the site of the North Middlesex Hospital.

Two

Hornsey High Street

The medieval church tower is at the highest point in Hornsey High Street near its easterly end. The shops which curve round to the church path are part of The Pavement, built in 1896. Originally the small village grouped near the church.

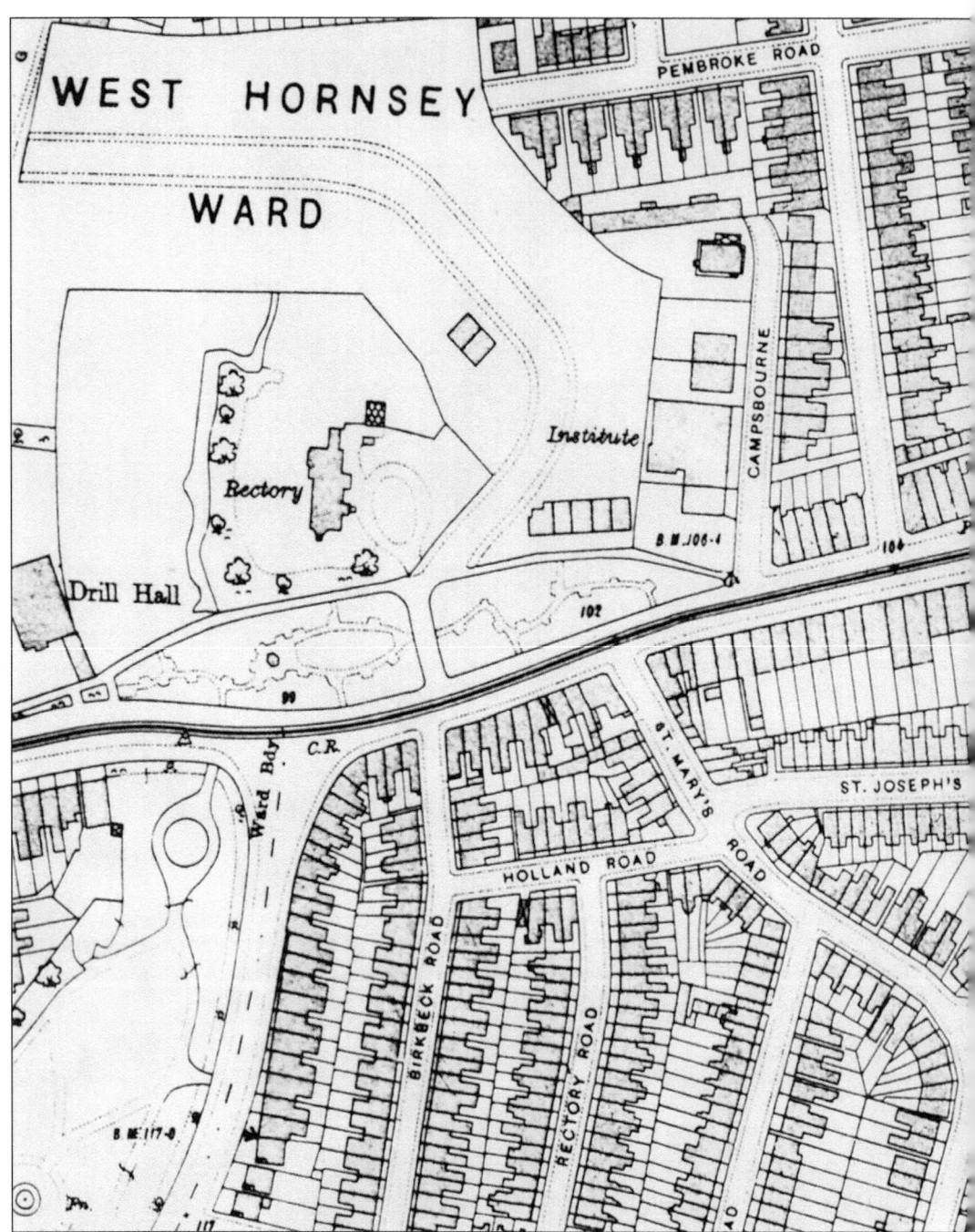

Hornsey High Street in 1912, showing the rectory at the western end and St Mary's church (both old and new) at the eastern end. Urban development of Hornsey village began at the western end on the Grove House estate on the south side and on the Campsbourne estate on the north side. These areas have both been redeveloped since the Second World War. Rectory Gardens encircles the rectory site where a church school has been built. The common land next to it remains. South of it are the Pleasure Gardens, abutting Middle Lane. The oldest buildings on the map are those opposite the church where Hornsey village had a cluster of cottages and The weatherboard cottage was the last of four wooden buildings which faced the common. In

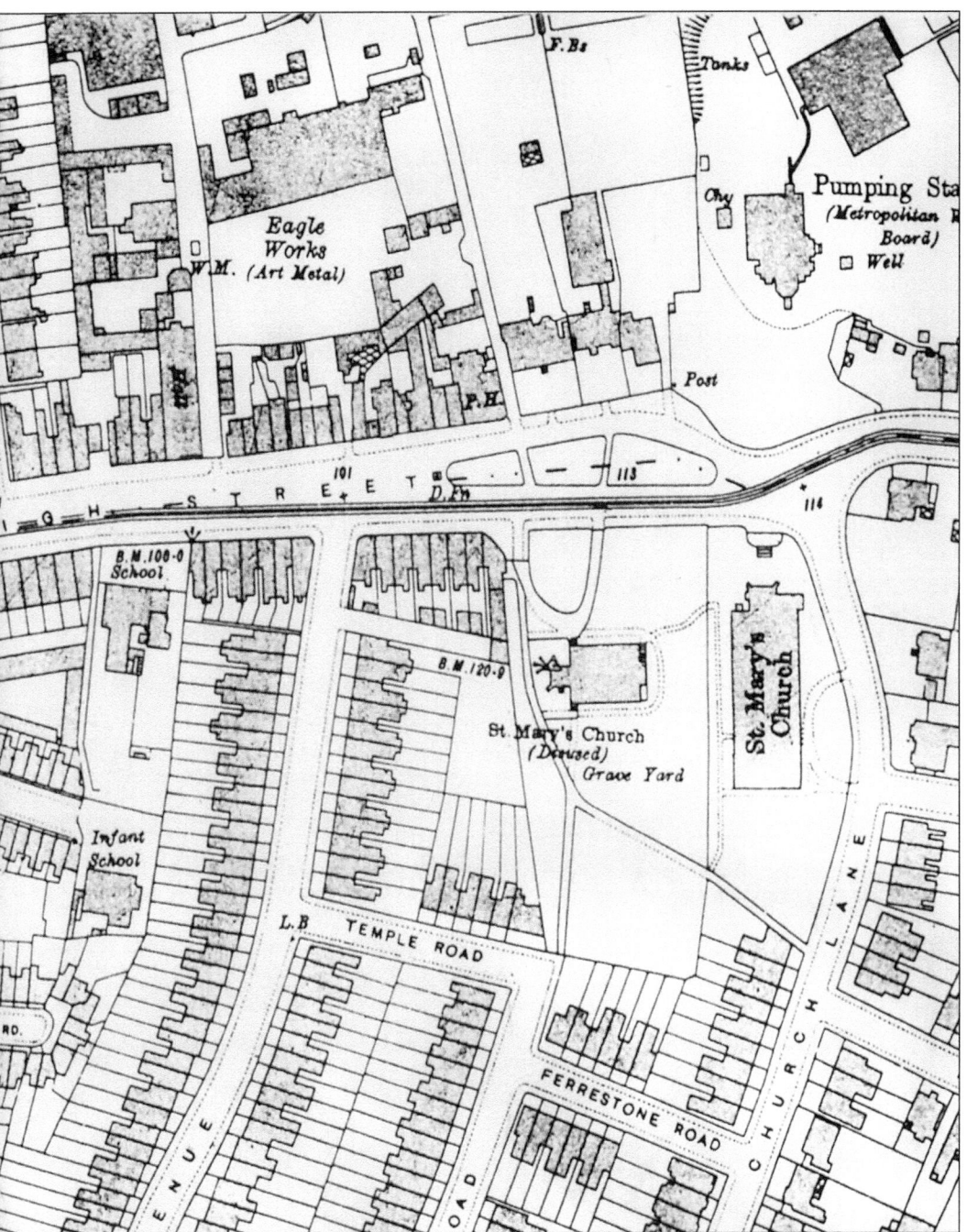

shops, plus some Georgian brick houses. The pumping station is on 9 acres acquired by the New River Company in 1854 under a private act of parliament. It bounds the Great Northern Railway main line which bridges the High Street at the east end. Lines along the High Street are the tram route. North west of Eagle Works, Hornsey Local Board in 1888 established a Sanitary Depot on a site bought for £13,296, which included a mortuary, coroner's court, fumigating plant, steam laundry and 217 ft chimney. In 1997 this site was targeted for sale and redevelopment. Glebe land south of the church was built over in the 1890s.

1891 Mrs Oakes, boot maker, was an occupant. The sign advertises boot repairs. The building was demolished around 1904.

With the cottage gone from view, from the same spot the waterworks' engine house (middle left) is visible, built in 1903 for the New River Company. Railings have gone from the common. This area of land, and the other at the western end of the High Street, were retained when enclosure awards dispensed with common land under the 1815 Hornsey Enclosure Act.

Looking west down the slope of the High Street with the railed common on the left. The eagle (right) is on a pillar outside No. 71 High Street.

In this view of the last weatherboard cottage some Georgian houses are to be seen. Eagle Court with the portico (left) survives, one of the oldest remaining houses in Hornsey.

Number 71 High Street, known as Eagle Court, was called Manor House in the nineteenth century. In 1908 it was taken over by Hornsey Young Men's Christian Assocation which built Parkinson Hall at the rear. Hornsey YMCA moved to a new building in Tottenham Lane in 1929.

Number 69 High Street, known as Eagle House, stands on the corner with Cross Lane. In the 1890s it was occupied by Jones and Willis, ecclesiastical furnishers, who manufactured art metal work in their Eagle Works north of the High Street. In the 1920s it was Hornsey Constitutional Club but by 1939 it had been divided into flats. It is one of the oldest local buildings, at one time occupied by the Cross family who gave their name to the adjoining lane.

The Great Northern Railway Tavern stands on the opposite corner of Cross Lane with the High Street. It is named after the Great Northern Railway, built nearby in 1850 with Hornsey as the first station out of London, and may have been the renaming of an earlier inn. It was rebuilt in 1897. Jones and Willis Art Metal Works sign is placed (right) over Cross Lane.

The Great Northern Railway Tavern was rebuilt for Cannon Brewery in 1897. The architect was Henry Whitebridge Rising of Shoebridge and Rising, who worked to high standards. Fine woodwork, glass and wrought iron work by Jones and Willis, the neighbouring firm, survive, and the date stone is retained on the side wall. The pub faces the church.

Hornsey High Street with The Great Northern Railway Tavern at the top of the rise, causing it to be referred to as the Top House. The weatherboard cottages and shops were almost swept away in the 1920s. The pillar (far left) marks the entrance road to the Sanitary Depot.

The same scene in about 1989 shows the pub and the three-storey brick premises, but the rest was replaced by car workshops and the council slipper baths.

Hornsey Public Baths and Wash Houses (Men and Women) were opened in 1932 as a one-storey building with the borough crest above the High Street doorway. In the 1950s the baths still had 33,000 users a year, benefiting those living in houses without bathrooms. It was later used for other purposes and in 1998 is threatened with demolition and redevelopment.

People assemble for a photograph outside the Half Price Stores. In the distance the cart belongs to Pye the fruiterer at No. 47. Preston's Court and Allen's Court were to the rear of the shops, all to be swept away in the 1920s with the baths built on the site.

Looking west down the High Street, still a muddy track in this Victorian view. Wooden railings line the common and the obelisk is to be seen in the distance.

The High Street with the yet to be rebuilt Great Northern Railway Tavern on 1 January 1890. The buildings, which might be late eighteenth century, contain a grocery provisions shop, a coffee room and dining rooms.

The obelisk drinking fountain was presented to Hornsey Parish in 1863 by Maria Hawes Ware of Middle Lane. In front of it is a granite trough given by the Metropolitan Drinking Fountain and Cattle Trough Association, providing water for horses and other livestock. The stone pillar is to prevent cart axle wheels damaging it. Some of these surviving troughs are used as flower beds but in 1994 this one had an neglected air.

In front of the obelisk stands a soldier, possibly seeking recruits for the First World War armies. It is probably 1914 for boot maker Peter Schwartz at No. 49 has draped a Union Jack in his window to show that, despite his German name, he is loyal to the crown. The tall brick building (right) is inscribed 'West London Dairy Company' and was probably built around 1900. A dairy occupied it until the 1930s.

Some thirty or so people are grouped outside Nos 19 and 21 Hornsey High Street in this summer photograph of 1905. This is the era of the small shop serving a local community. Not yet to be seen was the all-powerful motor vehicle which was to lead by the 1960s to shopping by car at supermarkets instead of at the local shop.

This fine group photograph is one of many taken by Alfred Braddock who turned professional in the 1880s, and in 1890 moved from Hackney to Hornsey, living finally at 120 Turnpike Lane. With his fine eye he recorded the local scene until about 1910, making a record of the last rural remnants as well as the new suburb.

Number 19 High Street, run by Mr Drew in 1905, (see previous photograph) had been taken over by Mrs Caroline Hackney by 1906. The empty premises at No. 21 with W.J. Miller's name was occupied by boot repairer William Saunders by 1912. Once again Braddock has people grouped for his photograph with a policeman joining in.

Eighty years later No. 21 is occupied by Ultra Communications. The space between terraces, occupied in 1906 by a Cash butchers shop, is now Myron Motor Centre. Now it is No. 21 which is the empty shop. Horse and cart have been replaced by an estate car.

Braddock has taken a closer view of Nos 19 and 21 High Street than in his photograph opposite. Some of the people are the same in both views, but a postman in his shako helmet stands prominently in front. Gas lamps illuminate the outside of the shops. Advertisements are for Cadbury's Chocolate and for Stephen's Ink. The newspaper posters talk of criminals, the mystery suicide of a millionaire's wife, betting, and football. A delivery bicycle leans against a tree.

The Three Compasses in 1892. On the south side of the High Street, this was a popular country pub, frequented by Londoners on a day out, with tea grounds, a cricket pitch and fishing in the New River which crossed the High Street three times until relocated in the mid nineteenth century.

The Three Compasses was rebuilt in 1896 to meet the needs of the now urbanized village. It continues today as a popular local public house.

THREE COMPASSES TAVERN & TEA GARDENS, HORNSEY

WILLIAM POULTON, *June 1860*

In calling attention to his

OLD ESTABLISHED TAVERN,

Where the public are supplied with every article of the best quality money can purchase, takes the opportuni of stating that, in addition to a variety of innocent amusements provided on the Grounds, the Visitors have opportunity of Fishing, &c.

Tea provided for any number, and every facility afforded for the enjoyment of his Patrons.

Were these the regulars assembled outside the rear of the old Three Compasses in 1860? All trades seem to represented, with a variety of headgear. William Poulton, the landlord for many years, was buried in the churchyard in a grave as near the pub as possible, at his own request, so that he could 'knock for his pint'. His gravestone is to be seen by the path nearest the pub. The parish vestry sometimes met in The Three Compasses. There were no buildings on the south side of the High Street between the pub and the church until a school was built in 1873.

Hornsey Tavern, on the south side of the High Street, was probably built in the 1860s when the National Freehold Land Company acquired the land behind and laid out six streets. It is 1906 and Alfred Braddock has assembled some seventy people for a group photograph.

Hornsey Tavern was rebuilt between the wars but still stands on the corner of St Mary's Road and the High Street. The streets behind were cleared and replaced by the new housing in the period between 1967 and 1976.

Numbers 14-24 Hornsey High Street, the terrace between St Mary's Road and Birbeck Road, with the Hornsey Tavern on the left. Passing people stop while Braddock takes his photograph, again in 1906. A typical perambulator of the period, now long out of use, can be seen. Walter Ham, fishmonger, at No. 14 will have an entry for the 1937 Coronation Carnival (see page 119).

Ninety years later the people have vanished but the terrace of shops, with Hornsey Tavern (left) the exception, remains much the same above ground level.

Numbers 78-90 Hornsey High Street, built 1896, with a date stone on the west side of Hillfield Avenue (left). A drapers shop, begun here by Mr A.J. Keens and Mr E.C. Van de Vord, became by 1912 Keevans Stores and occupied four adjacent shops. They closed in December 1988 after ninety-one years here.

St Mary's School in 1976, just before demolition. The site was used first for a church school in 1873, with rebuilding taking place in 1929 with funding from David Greig. An infants' school was at the rear (see map, pages 20-21). The school site is now occupied by St David's and St Katherine's School.

Numbers 66-76 High Street on the west side of the school site have been demolished and the land incorporated into the playground of St David's and St Katherine's School, forming a gap in the High Street. In 1905 Braddock took a group photograph, this time with many children.

St Mary's Terrace of three shops was built in 1870 on the corner of St Mary's Road. Number 32 (Universal Travel) was where the Greig family began to sell home made foods. One son, David Greig, was to build a national chain of provision stores which survived until 1972. Numbers 32 and 34 were to form a branch; distinctive tiling is still to be seen outside. David Greig charitable trusts help fund local church schools and educational work.

Birkbeck Road, laid out over the Grove House estate on the corner of High Street and Middle Lane by the Birkbeck Freehold Land Company from 1866. Neighbouring land, owned by John Holland (after whom a road was named), had been bought in 1865 by the National Freehold Land Company. Many of the roads have been dispensed with in post-war rebuilding. Birkbeck Road survives on its westerly side.

Lightfoot Road slopes down to Middle Lane. The National Freehold Land Company named it after Biblical critic John Lightfoot (1602-75) who lived in Hornsey. Lightfoot was an Anglican minister who became Vice-Chancellor of Cambridge University.

This pair of villas was built in Campsbourne near the High Street, c.1870. By 1911 it was used by the Baptists and named The Institute. A Baptist church and church hall were built on the north side in 1906. Campsbourne and parallel Campsbourne Road take their name from the medieval estate which encompassed the Campsbourne (or Moselle) River.

Electric trams began to run along Hornsey High Street in 1905. The service ran from Turnpike Lane to the foot of Muswell Hill, with single deckers going to Alexandra Palace. This view was taken by Braddock not in winter but in April 1908 at Easter.

Hornsey High Street ends at Middle Lane. In this 1890 view the opposite corner is occupied by Ivy Lodge, which vanished when the public recreation ground was created soon afterwards on its site.

Middle Lane is an ancient route once known as Freeze Lane. Palace Road is the turning on the left and on the right are Elm House and Rokesly House. These two survived until 1934, forming a green barrier, with their estates, between Hornsey and Crouch End villages.

Three

Nightingale Lane

Nightingale Cottage on the corner of Nightingale Lane and Priory Road in 1893 when it was occupied by William Hayden. The sign directs travellers to the pub in Nightingale Lane. In 1899 the cottage was replaced by a terrace of seven shops, which still stands.

The Nightingale was a country pub in the nineteenth century, frequented by holiday-making Londoners and famous for its quoits and tea garden. Fishing could be had in the New River and in the Campsbourne, which flowed north of the High Street.

The Nightingale was rebuilt in 1896, responding like the other Hornsey country pubs to urbanization. Modernized in 1997, The Nightingale still operates in Nightingale Lane.

Nightingale Lane in 1894, with the group of cottages known as Nightingale Place dating from 1851. They were demolished in 1896. Nightingale Lane led to a field called Campsbourne, acquired in 1897 by Hornsey Urban District Council for housing over which Northview and Southview Roads were laid out. Campsbourne School, built at the north end of Nightingale Lane, celebrated its centenary in 1997. Hawthorne and Beechwood Roads were added from 1906.

Nightingale Place comprised fourteen cottages north of the Nightingale pub. Some of them were of wooden construction.

The rear of The Nightingale in 1898. Families could come here and take refreshments.

Four

Alexandra Palace
and Park

Nightingale Lane led to former farmland which in 1863 was acquired for Alexandra Park and the building of Alexandra Palace. The parish boundary with Tottenham crossed the top of Nightingale Lane, but much of the southern portion of the park was in Hornsey. The card depicts the second palace of 1875.

The second Alexandra Palace opened in 1875. The first palace had been built by 1866 but did not open until 1873 when it almost immediately burnt down. This 1875 building was hit by a disastrous fire in July 1980. It was partly restored and reopened in 1988.

The Great Hall of the 1875 palace was 386 ft long, 184 ft wide and designed to seat over 12,000 people. The Willis organ outstripped in size, design and equipment any other in the country. The hall was used for musical events, political gatherings, circuses, exhibitions and other displays.

Belgian refugees were housed in 1914-15 in the palace while seeking accommodation in the UK. Here they are in the roller skating rink, which was then located in the north west corner.

The picture saloon at Alexandra Palace contained a changing display of works of art. Also located in the palace was the collection of arms and armour formed by Lord Londesborough.

The Monkey House and Zoological Collection were popular attractions within the palace.
Admission was one (old) penny for the zoo which was a collection of small animals.

The conservatory was at the western end of the palace and is known as the Palm Court today.
Tropical trees were grown.

This aerial view from the early 1930s shows the palace before the British Broadcasting Corporation erected a mast in 1935 on the south east corner in preparation for television transmissions. This resulted in 1936 in the world's first regular high definition public television service. Set on a 305 ft hill, the site for a people's palace to rival Crystal Palace had been chosen in 1858 by architect Owen Jones. A heavy brick and stone building was eventually put up instead of the glass one envisaged by Jones. 'Since its opening in 1875', said a 1905 guidebook, 'it has had a career of intermittent unprosperity as if the Graces and Muses had combined to punish the crime of loading such a site with such a unlovely structure'. A place for fine views, it can be seen from afar. The racecourse, reservoirs of the water company, and Northview Road at the top of Nightingale Lane can be seen.

Alexandra Park hosted many entertainments and sporting events, included fun fairs and this giant switchback. The racecourse lasted from 1868 to 1970. Trams were replaced by buses in 1938 on a road connecting the Hornsey and Wood Green entrances, which now runs through the park, and carries other traffic.

The Grove, where concerts have always been held, was the estate of an ancient mansion called The Grove, entered from Muswell Hill. It was acquired in 1863 when the farm was purchased to make the park. The house was demolished in about 1870. A bandstand and tea room were provided.

Five

Priory Road

The headquarters of the 1st Middlesex Volunteer Battalion of the Duke of Cambridge's Own was in the former Elm House, in Priory Road, on the corner of Nightingale Lane. It had been purchased in 1896 and was replaced in 1900 by a Drill Hall. This in turn has been rebuilt as a Territorial Army headquarters. Elm House, with twelve bedrooms, had stood in 1¾acres.

Priory Road still ran through green fields at the latter end of the nineteenth century. It was lined by the paling fence and mature trees of the Warner family's Priory estate, which was on each side of the wide road.

The horse rider could be a member of the Warner family or another local estate owner, though by 1900 when it was taken the Warner family had moved away and most estates had gone.

Opposite The Elms, just past Middle Lane, stood Lindsay Cottages, The Ferns and Ashford House. The cottages went in the 1890s when the Pleasure Grounds were created and the site was used for a toilet block. Ashford House and grounds went in the 1900s, replaced by Oak and Ashford Avenues. The Ferns escaped demolition. This photograph dates from 1892.

Ferns House in Priory Road still bears the marks on its side wall where Lindsay Cottages abutted it. For a time the house was a private school. The toilet block (left) has been converted into private residence, following its sale. The terrace (right) dates from about 1910.

The Priory stood on the north side of Priory Road in some 18 acres, acquired in 1796 by London grocer Jacob Warner. Designed by William Pocock in the 1820s in Gothic revival style, it incorporated panelling and doors taken from Wanstead House, Essex, then being demolished. It survived until 1902.

Henry Reader Williams (1822-1897) occupied the mansion in the 1890s after the Warners had moved away. A wine merchant and philanthropist, he was for nearly twenty-two years Chairman of Hornsey Local Board until 1894, when it was superseded by Hornsey Urban District Council. Crouch End Clock Tower was erected in his honour two years before his death.

Rear view of The Priory, which had substantial outbuildings including a probably older stable block with a tower and clock. The extensive grounds were used for inspections of the local Middlesex Volunteers, Henry Warner being Lieutenant Colonel of the 2nd Battalion. When he died in 1883 the family ceased to live in The Mansion. After H.R. Williams died in 1897, the estate was developed with avenues of tall, well built terraced houses designed by architect and surveyor John Farrer. No connection with any priory on the site has been established.

Trams ran along Priory Road from 1905 until 1938 when they were replaced by buses. The parade of seven shops (left) on the corner of Nightingale Lane continues to trade. They were built in 1899.

Priory Road, Hornsey.

Priory Road developed into a fairly wide thoroughfare with some remaining grass verges, surrounded by well built Edwardian properties, with parkland on its south side. The only shopping terraces were at each end by Nightingale Lane and Park Road.

Hornsey National School for Boys, or St Mary's, was established on the north side of Priory Road in about 1819 and enlarged in 1850. As the population rapidly expanded it moved in 1873 into Hornsey High Street. The former school buildings were not demolished but went into private occupancy. In 1891 Mrs Preston, a laundress, lived in Old Hornsey School and Edwin Rowbottam in Old School Cottage. In this 1898 view, houses have already joined it on the east side, but had only just been built. The school buildings were demolished soon after. They were located where Priory Avenue is now.

The Recreation or Pleasure Grounds, were established in 1891 on land purchased from Colonel Henry Warner and his relative, Mr Linzee, by Hornsey Local Board. They were opened to the public in 1894. The Metcalf Fountain (left) was moved here from Crouch End Broadway in 1895. It had been given in 1879 by Thomas Page Metcalf as a replacement for the village pump.

Priory Road was lined with houses on the north side by 1912, but on the south side 9 acres known as Lewcock's Field, owned by a local builder, were undeveloped. In 1926 these were added to the Pleasure Grounds and the whole renamed Priory Park.

The original 8 acres of the Pleasure Grounds were to prove an attractive facility for the residents of the newly built Priory Estate. In addition to the Metcalf Fountain, left, another larger fountain was added in 1909. Weighing 50 tons it came from St Paul's Cathedral churchyard and bears the arms of the City of London and of the bishop; it was an appropriate acquisition as the Bishop of London was lord of the manor of Hornsey. A gatekeeper's cottage was erected in the 1890s on land purchased in Barrington Road by Hornsey Local Board. This view looks north, with Middle Lane out of sight on the right.

Alexandra Palace, Hornsey

Alexandra Palace can be seen from Priory Park as shown by this view, taken at the beginning of the twentieth century from what were then the Pleasure Grounds.

The interior of St George's church, built on the south side of Priory Road in 1907 to serve the new population. Designed by J.S. Alder, architect of St James's, Muswell Hill, and many other London churches, it stood on the corner of Park Avenue South. Bombed in 1940 it was demolished in 1956 and a new church built in Cranley Gardens. The site was taken in 1963 for a new Hornsey fire station.

Carriage roads were built between the houses and Priory Road known as East Drive and West Drive. Plans for the estate were submitted to Hornsey Urban District Council in 1899 by architect John Farrer. Left is No. 98 Priory Road, named the Priory as it now stands on part of the site of the original house. It is now sheltered accommodation with extensions built in the 1980s.

Newly built Priory Avenue in 1907, one of the Edwardian avenues laid out on the north side of Priory Road. Hornsey Council planted many trees on roads throughout the borough. Many mature trees were lost when new housing estates were built.

Racegoers in cabs leaving Alexandra Park. This entrance to the park at the end of Priory Road was on leased ground created to afford access to the 1868 racetrack. The Priory Road house, right, survives. In 1911 the houses were yet to be numbered.

Looking south from the park entrance in 1890. Priory Road is to the left and Park Road ahead, leading to Crouch End. The area is still rural, one of the last, with Muswell Hill, to remain so in Hornsey at this date. Rose Cottage opposite, behind the signpost, was replaced in 1902 by a shopping parade.

Five or six wooden cottages stood at the end of Priory Road in 1890, captured by Braddock before their disappearance. One of the occupants was George Friend and they were known as Friend's Cottages. (Before systematic road naming and numbering farms and houses were often named after their occupants.) The inhabitants offered light refreshments to those visiting Alexandra Park, an entrance to which was nearby. To the right is the site of the parish pound used for keeping stray animals; the site was later used by the local authority for public toilets, (empty in the 1990s and disused). In this view Braddock has included a postman and policeman.

Priory Road ends at the foot of steep Muswell Hill, with Park Road leading to Crouch End (left) and an entrance to Alexandra Park (right). This Edwardian view shows a neat road junction with the signpost still in place.

In this 1950s view of the road junction, alterations have been made to accommodate motorized road traffic. Traffic signals will be installed in due course to control the flow. The Buckingham Lodge block of flats now overlooks the scene.

Muswell Hill is an ancient route to the north (via Colney Hatch Lane). Estates lined its sides, of which only (rebuilt) Grove Lodge estate with entrance lodge remain. The trees (right) were saved after the Second World War when Hornsey Council purchased the land there.

The Moravian church in Priory Road dates from 1907. The Moravian Episcopal Free Church orginated in central Europe in the fifteenth century. Its British headquarters is now at Nos 3 and 5 Muswell Hill, early nineteenth century houses acquired in 1957, the year the church celebrated its 500th anniversary. Its headquarters in Fetter Lane were bombed in 1940 and moved temporarily to Onslow Gardens.

No. 1160.   *Playing Fields looking towards, Muswell Hill.*

Crouch End Playing Fields lie on the flatter land below Muswell Hill, on the western side of Park Road. Land was first leased here from the church, originally part of its medieval Rowledge Farm, in 1893 by a Playing Fields Company established by Ernest Hindley, son-in-law to H.R. Williams.

NORTH MIDDLESEX CRICKET CLUB

The Playing Fields Company eventually purchased the freehold and by 1956 there were 53 acres of playing fields held by the company and in active use by many private cricket and lawn tennis clubs. Land between the playing fields and Park Road was given by the church for Hornsey Cottage Hospital, opened in 1910 and later extended. Next to it in Park Road a swimming pool was opened by the council in 1929 with an indoor pool added in 1975.

Six

Tottenham Lane

Tottenham Lane with the police station, library and fire station (right) standing next to each other on the crest of the hill. Tottenham Lane is part of an ancient route between Crouch End and Hornsey and the parish of Tottenham. It rises from Crouch End to this crest then continues downhill to Hornsey High Street.

LIBRARY & FIRE STATION HORNSEY

The police station (1884), the public library (1899) and the fire station (1885) formed a civic centre between Hornsey village and Crouch End as the area was urbanized. The local authority remained in Southwood Lane offices, Highgate. Rebuilt in 1915 and later refurbished, the police station survives and has taken over the whole site. The library was replaced in 1965 and the fire station in 1963, with buildings elsewhere.

1171   Tottenham Lane & Fire Station. Hornsey

Looking north from the crest with Church Lane running downhill ahead and Tottenham Lane continuing downhill on the right, to pass Hornsey railway station and yards. Hornsey sorting office is opposite Hornsey railway station. At the centre are Ferrestone Buildings built at the end of the nineteenth century on Ferrestone Lodge estate.

70

St Mary's School for Girls (right) moved to Tottenham Lane on glebe land in 1832 with an infants' school built near it in 1848 (replaced by an infants' school behind the boys' Hornsey High Street School in 1884). From 1929 both boys and girls used a new High Street School, leaving this school to the infants. It was demolished in the 1970s after a new St Mary's Infants' School opened in Church Lane on the church site. In this 1906 view Church Hill Cottages, a row of six, are on the left.

Hoardings surrounded the site of the demolished school until in the 1990s, Haringey redeveloped it for housing, named Elmcroft after a former nearby estate. This 1990 view shows the school railings in position. They remain in place now that housing has replaced the hoarding. Hornsey Police Station in the distance stands on the corner of Harold Road.

The Hope and Anchor, a country pub in Tottenham Lane not far from St Mary's School, photographed by Braddock, before rebuilding at the end of the nineteenth century.

The Hope and Anchor (left) kept its name after rebuilding until the 1990s when it was renamed The Orange Kipper. The tree next to it is in the estate of the Old Chestnuts, a doctor's house next to another villa called Elmcroft. The pub faces shopping parades and roads built by John Cathles Hill. Millman Terrace is dated 1889.

The Abyssinian, demolished in 1968, served the Hornsey Vale enclave off Tottenham Lane. Its name has been said to have come from wild people called Abyssinians when the pub was built in 1890. The pub sign erected in 1945 depicted Prince Monolulu, the racing tipster. Building was halted at two storeys in 1890 by Wenlock Brewery because licensing magistrates would only grant a wine and beer licence, claiming it replaced an off-licence. A full licence was not granted until 1948.

Enfield Gardens was on the Hornsey Vale estate. This urban enclave was laid out in the 1870s and 1880s and had a village atmosphere. Houses on the six roads were cleared by compulsory purchase order during 1968. The site is now occupied by Hornsey Comprehensive School for Girls.

Holy Innocents' was built in Tottenham Lane on glebe land, 1876-77. The architect was Arthur Blomfield (1822-1899) son of a Bishop of London; he designed Christ Church, Crouch End and the Royal College of Music, Kensington. The design was in the Gothic style in yellow and red brick to seat 800. A vicarage was built behind. It was one of six daughter churches to St Mary's parish church.

St Mary's Upper Grade School in Tottenham Lane in the Edwardian period. The boys', girls' and infants' departments were classed as Upper Grade by 1899 but regarded as one school from 1905.

Built on glebe land in 1848 as Hornsey National Infants' School, this was renamed Holy Innocents' School (infants) in 1885 following the opening the previous year of St Mary's Infants' School. When in 1934 Rokesly Avenue Infants' School opened nearly opposite it closed. An annexe and the schoolmistress's house were demolished and the remainder made into a shelter. After conversion it reopened in 1981 as Hornsey Historical Society's HQ, renamed The Old School House.

This group of thirty-six were pupils at Holy Innocents' Infants' School, *c.* 1930. Past pupils have been welcome guests at functions run by the Hornsey Historical Society in recent years. This group of children were the generation which grew up to serve in the Second World War.

Kitchener House was built in Hillfield Avenue in 1905 as Carleton House at the south west end and was occupied by a Lord Mayor of London. By 1920 it was Kitchener Home for boys, funded from the memorial fund for the war leader, Lord Kitchener, drowned in 1916. After the Second World War it became Kitchener Training College. In 1997 it was redeveloped by the Metropolitan Home Ownership into flats, with a block of flats also built in the grounds.

Hillfield Avenue was laid out over glebe land when the Rector of Hornsey finally decided to allow building, in the 1890s. Nearby Rokesly House, Hermitage Lodge and Elm Lodge estates also resisted building developments, separating Hornsey from Crouch End. Trees were planted by Hornsey Urban District Council in new roads.

Hillfield Avenue, once known as Hillyfield, was laid out south from the High Street to connect with Holy Innocents Road; this short road led past Holy Innocents School to Tottenham Lane. In 1912 Holy Innocents Road was made part of Rokesly Avenue, laid out when Hermiston Lodge estate was sold for development. This view of Hillfield Avenue was photographed by Braddock around 1905.

Hillfield Avenue in the 1990s looks much the same as in 1905. The retention of the wooden period window frames and doors is an important aspect of conservation. One individual house owner who makes ill-informed alterations can spoil the look of a road.

Five houses of three storeys known as Manor Cottages, and eight of two storeys known as Manor Place, stood in Tottenham Lane opposite Ferme Park Road (built in the 1880s). Much photographed as a picturesque feature, they were either seventeenth or eighteenth century in origin. They were all demolished in 1935 as part of Hornsey Council's clearance programme. Number 1 Manor Cottages (left) was occupied by a builder; a chimney sweep, wardrobe dealer and a general smith were among the occupiers of the other premises.

The site of Manor Place is occupied by derelict garages shielded from Tottenham Lane by these hoardings. The site of Manor Cottages is now occupied by a garage and filling station.

Beyond the old cottages in this view can be seen the white bulk of Hornsey YMCA, opened in 1929. A steel-framed building designed by Capt. Harold Burley RIBA, it was built on a site donated by Mr A.B. Cloutman, director of Maples furnishing company, who was a member of nearby Ferme Park Baptist Church (founded 1889, demolished 1973, replaced 1980).

Hornsey YMCA remains on site but the original 1929 building, extended in 1959, was remodelled in the 1990s. The number of bedrooms has been increased from 57 to 158 and more recreational facilities provided. Its restaurant is open to the public. The building stands between Elmsfield Avenue and Rosebery Gardens.

Manor Cottages (left) and the Salvation Army Hostel (right) in this view of Tottenham Lane. The hostel has a foundation stone laid in 1912 by popular novelist Silas K. Hocking, who lived in Avenue Road, Crouch End. The hostel was built on the site of Lightcliffe House. The trees next to it are in the front garden of Alresford Lodge, home of a surgeon. The terrace of shops beyond, built in 1889, was named Victoria Terrace.

The Salvation Army Hostel is the Hustler Snooker Club in this 1994 view and Alresford Lodge the site of a petrol station. Opposite is the petrol station built on the site of Manor Cottages. Holy Innocents' church survives on the rising ground beyond.

Victoria Terrace shops spread their goods out onto the pavement of Tottenham Lane in this Edwardian view. The plaque on the corner of Ferme Park Road (middle right) is labelled Clarke's Buildings 1889.

The southern end of Tottenham Lane was transformed in the 1890s when developers John Cathles Hill and James Edmondson built new shopping parades on each side of it. The date stone 1895 is to be seen on Topsfield Parade on the corner of Elder Avenue. The parade was built by Edmondson on the site of the Topsfield Hall estate.

The Queen's Opera House was incorporated by Edmondson into Topsfield Parade at No. 31. Opened in 1897, it was later renamed the Hippodrome and mostly used as a cinema until bombed in the Second World War. The auditorium was then demolished and became a mail order firm headquarters with an ungainly dark glass façade. In 1997 it was remodelled as a fitness gym with the stained glass restored.

The Queens at No. 26 Broadway Parade, nearly opposite the Opera House, was built in 1899 on the corner of Elder Avenue, by John Cathles Hill. Temperance Movement opposition delayed licensing until 1901. Like the Salisbury Hotel in Green Lanes, which Hill also built, the building was opulently furnished. Much of the period detail survives.

Topsfield Parade (left), built by Edmondson, is faced by Broadway Parade (right), built by Hill. The row of thirty-eight shops by Hill continued beyond the Queen's Hotel and Elder Avenue to terminate in Tottenham Lane at the Picture House. This cinema stood opposite Rosebery Gardens and was built in 1911. Later known as the Plaza, it was bombed in the Second World War. Although both parades survive the road is now filled with motorised traffic.

Middle Lane, which joins Tottenham Lane at the Broadway, contains at Nos 9-35 a terrace of small cottage houses grouped in pairs dating from around 1850, a period when village development increased in Crouch End. The houses have the kind of Italianate decoration more usually applied to larger houses, including stuccoed angles with upper pilasters and brackets. In 1997, Nos 21 and 23 collapsed during building work but have since been rebuilt.

Park Road joins Middle Lane and contains (right) surviving 1850s properties with No. 8 named Aberdeen House, probably as a tribute to Lord Aberdeen, Prime Minister 1852-55. Previously known as Maynard Street, the thoroughfare was renamed Park Road after the opening of Alexandra Park at the far end in 1863. Hornsey School Board built in 1893 an extension to Crouch End School in Park Road adjacent to its 1877 school in Wolseley Road. In 1994 most of the school buildings were replaced by housing development.

This mid-nineteenth-century building on the corner of Park Road and Middle Lane still stands. Occupied from 1852 for a considerable period by a corn merchants later known as Forbes Boden & Co., it met the needs of the neighbourhood when it was still agricultural and horse transport required feed. Edmund Field, standing by the horse, became manager of Boden's other shop at 49 Park Road.

Seven

Crouch End Broadway

Crouch End Broadway in celebratory mood, possibly commemorating the coronation of Edward in 1902. By then the Broadway had become an important shopping centre for the new suburb. But despite urbanization it has always retained the atmosphere of a village centre, aided by its geographical position in a valley.

Topsfield Hall stood at the junction of Tottenham Lane and Middle Lane. Traditionally the manor house for Topsfield Manor, it was a late Georgian building which survived until 1894. Land belonging to the estate was sold in 1882 when occupant Henry Weston Elder, a London bristle merchant, died. The house and the rest of the land were sold after the death in 1892 of his widow.

Topsfield Hall servants in 1880, when the youngest daughter of the house married Frank May, Chief Cashier to the Bank of England. Henry Weston Elder gave his daughter a carriage and pair as a wedding present.

Crouch Hall was built in 1820 on the west side of the Broadway by the Booth family as a better home than Old Crouch Hall of 1681 on the east side of the road. The Booths were gin distillers and were followed by William Bird, iron merchant, in 1859. When the house was sold in 1882 it was said that 'the birds had flown'.

The purchaser of the Crouch Hall estate was the Imperial Property Investment Company which laid out Crouch Hall Road and others. The company also purchased the adjacent Crouch End Academy, situated on the bend into Park Road. Founded in 1613, this boarding school brought vitality to the village; the Academy building was demolished in 1882. By 1891 some sixty houses had been built on the Crouch Hall estate.

Topsfield Hall is just to be seen in this view of Crouch End Broadway taken before its demolition in 1894. Shopping parades have been erected (left) on the Crouch Hall estate (purchased 1882, house demolished a few years later). Opposite stand Bank Buildings of 1887. The Metcalf Fountain, here from 1879 to 1895, is on the right.

BROADWAY CROUCH END.

Topsfield Hall has gone in this view. The Pavement, Topsfield Parade and the Clock Tower, all of 1895, have taken its place. Awnings were popular with shop keepers to shield their goods from the sun.

The Clock Tower viewed from Crouch Hall Road. The medallion commemorating H.R. Williams, designed by Alfred Gilbert (the sculptor of the statue of Eros in Piccadilly Circus) can be seen. The Clock Tower was designed by F.G. Knight with a granite base surmounted by stripes of red and yellow Mansfield stone. The upper part of red brick is crowned by a terracotta cupola. It was unveiled on 22 June 1895, in Williams's lifetime, in his honour. Behind it can be seen the name of another Williams who ran a creamery at No. 48 Broadway, on the corner of Weston Park. This attractive, turreted corner building survives and in 1998 was in use as a restaurant.

THE CLOCK TOWER, CROUCH END.

The north and west sides of the Clock Tower in 1904 are uncluttered. Underground toilets would be built next to it in 1925 (removed in 1996) and an island was added as traffic increased, as well as traffic signals. The centenary of the Clock Tower was the occasion of closing the Broadway and holding a festival in June 1995.

Looking south from the Clock Tower towards Criterion Buildings, and the fork of Crouch Hill and Crouch End Hill. Large street gas lamps adorned the pavements in the first few years of the twentieth century. Busy shops include that of James Wilson, far right.

James H. Wilson moved his small drapery business from Park Road to No. 39 the Broadway, on the corner of Crouch Hall Road, in 1886. By 1939 the business occupied Nos 23-39 and was the leading department store. Councillor Wilson fought for better conditions for shop workers, including early closing.

Wilson's suffered from incendiary bomb raids in February 1944 but continued to operate until 1971, when the group which owned it ceased trading. The rebuilt corner site contained a branch of Woolworths from 1957 and the remainder was rebuilt with a glass façade and incorporated a supermarket.

Weston Park near the Broadway was laid out in 1888 after Sarah Elder had agreed to the demolition of Old Crouch Hall and adjacent Linslade House. Large semi-detached houses were designed by architect J. Farrer. The eastern end of Weston Park had been developed earlier in the 1880s with Ferme Park Baptist Church built on its corner with Ferme Park Road. Its dome can be seen here (since demolished and the church rebuilt).

Lake Villa, set back from the Broadway, was built early in the nineteenth century in the grounds of Old Crouch Hall. It was demolished in 1924 and its site, along with neighbouring Broadway Hall or Chapel, cleared, to be used in the 1930s for the town hall complex. Dr Frederic Orton, Hornsey Medical Officer for Health, lived in it from at least 1889 until 1920. It is probably his carriage seen here.

Salute the Soldier parade held in March 1944 after allied victories in Italy. St John's Ambulance
Brigade cadets pass the saluting base with Alderman H.G.J. Williams OBE, Mayor of Hornsey,
among those present. Numbers 17-39 Broadway are seen on the left, showing how they were
before post-war redevelopment.

THE NEW TOWN HALL, HORNSEY. 257.

Hornsey Town Hall, opened on 4 November 1935 by the Duke of Kent, replaced local authority offices in Highgate built in 1869. The architect was New Zealander Reginald Uren (1906-88) and the building won the RIBA bronze medal for the best London building 1933-35. The brick, L-shaped building with tower ceased being a town hall in 1965 when Haringey was formed. Left is to be seen the telephone exchange, later relocated on Crouch End Hill.

The gas showrooms, flanking the town hall on the south side, were built in 1935-37 by architects Dawe and Carter. Stone panels beneath the windows depict gas industry scenes and were carved in low relief by Arthur Ayres. The north side of the town hall forecourt contained the electricity showrooms. The gas building became Barclays Bank in about 1990.

The electricity showrooms are to be seen on the right in this post-war view of the Broadway. The building was adapted in 1937-39 from the former telephone exchange on the site by architects Slater, Moberly and Uren. A brick relief by Arthur Ayres of the Spirit of Electricity is above the office entrance. On the left Tesco has displaced J. Lyons, on the corner with Coleridge Road since 1924.

Dunn's the bakers is at No. 6 Broadway, adjacent to the gas showroom building. The two-storey yellow stock brick building is ornamented with a bold cornice crowned by a wheatsheaf over the date 1850 and the initials 'W.M'. These stood for William Muddiman, whose bakery and post office appears in directories for most of a century and maintain a very popular business.

This smithy stood at the southern end of the Broadway at the foot of Crouch End Hill, occupied in 1890 by farrier Charles Batterby. Left is Chapel Place on Crouch Hill, a terrace of five shops with No. 5 occupied by William Underwood, family butcher, abutting the smithy, which was replaced after the death of Sarah Elder of Topsfield Hall in 1894, owner of the site.

Crouch Hill, with Criterion Buildings on the right which replaced Chapel Place and the smithy on this corner. Number 1 is occupied by the London and Westminster Bank, later to take over the whole of the building. The spire is of Park Chapel.

Eight

Crouch Hill

Crouch Hill in the 1920s looking down towards the Broadway. Haringey Terrace of nine shops on the right, named after Haringey Park, the road on which the corner shop stands, was already trading in 1889. Opposite No. 153 Crouch Hill has always been listed in Kelly's directory as a beer sellers, though it carries the signboard of The Harringay Arms.

Criterion Buildings at the junction of Crouch Hill and Crouch End Hill in 1937. The London and Westminster Bank became the London, County and Westminster and then in 1923 the Westminster Bank. From occupying only No. 1 Criterion Buildings, the branch took it all over in 1935. It then rebuilt the site. The Westminster Bank took over the National Provincial in 1962 and was renamed NatWest in 1970. In 1996 this branch celebrated one hundred years on the site.

Hornsey Central Library, opened in Haringey Park in 1965, was designed by F. Ley and G. Jarvis. The staircase has a large window with engravings of Hornsey's historical buildings by F.J. Mitchell. A fountain with a bronze sculpture stands on the corner with Hatherley Gardens, which leads to the town hall. Haringey Park was laid out in 1855 with large houses, some of which survive, Crouch End's first residential middle class road.

Park Congregational Chapel, facing Haringey Park, was founded in 1854. The original Gothic stone building was built with the small spire. Extended four times it could eventually seat 1,400. Left is Hornsey 'British' nonconformist church school, replaced in 1892 by Corbin Hall.

Park Chapel with ivy-covered Corbin Hall on the left. The church gave up the building in the 1970s when Congregationalists merged with Presbyterians to form the United Reformed Church. Subsequently it has been used commercially, mostly for filming (including animated puppet films) and for recording popular music, a function which has drawn world celebrities such as Bob Dylan to Crouch End.

Cecile House at 104 Crouch Hill was built in 1865. The first occupant was George Shadbolt (1819-1901) a pioneer photographer who took views of Hornsey in the 1860s whilst working for the family firm of mahogany brokers. In 1892 a road was built alongside the house by J. Farrer on the Elder family lands and named Cecile Park. By this time the house had become a ladies' school and in 1939 was a school of dancing.

Cecile House was occupied after the Second World War by Peter Coxhead who, with Ralph Nossek and David Angus, founded the Mountview repertory theatre (taking the name from the local telephone exchange). Success as a drama school led to the premises being expanded. With patronage from leading theatre figures and of national standing, it is due to take over halls in the Town Hall. It moved out in 2007.

Crouch Hill at the junction with Cecile Park (right) and Christchurch Road (left), with Park Chapel in the distance. An air of gentility pervades the scene. Little has changed except that the pillar box has been moved further to the left, probably to aid collections.

Number 113 Crouch Hill, a late Victorian house on the corner of Haslemere Road. Its decorative terracotta plaques, tall chimneys and elaborate gables derive from the picturesque motifs used by contemporary architects such as Norman Shaw. Occupied by a doctor in 1911, in the 1990s it is the Red Gables Family Centre, run by the council to aid those with young children.

CROUCH HILL N.

Crouch Hill ascends to a ridge known locally as the 'Hogs Back'. These upper slopes were known as Mount Pleasant and afforded fine views either north to Alexandra Palace or south over London. This shows its descent on the south side towards Stroud Green, with Crouch Hill station at the foot of Crouch Hill to be reached.

Holly Park, Crouch Hill

Holly Park, on the east side of Crouch Hill, was a residential estate with entrance gates which were formally closed once a year. It had been built from 1864 in the grounds of a house called The Hollies. Post war, the estate was redeveloped by Islington (within whose area it lay) as a municipal housing project.

Nine

Crouch End Hill and Hornsey Lane

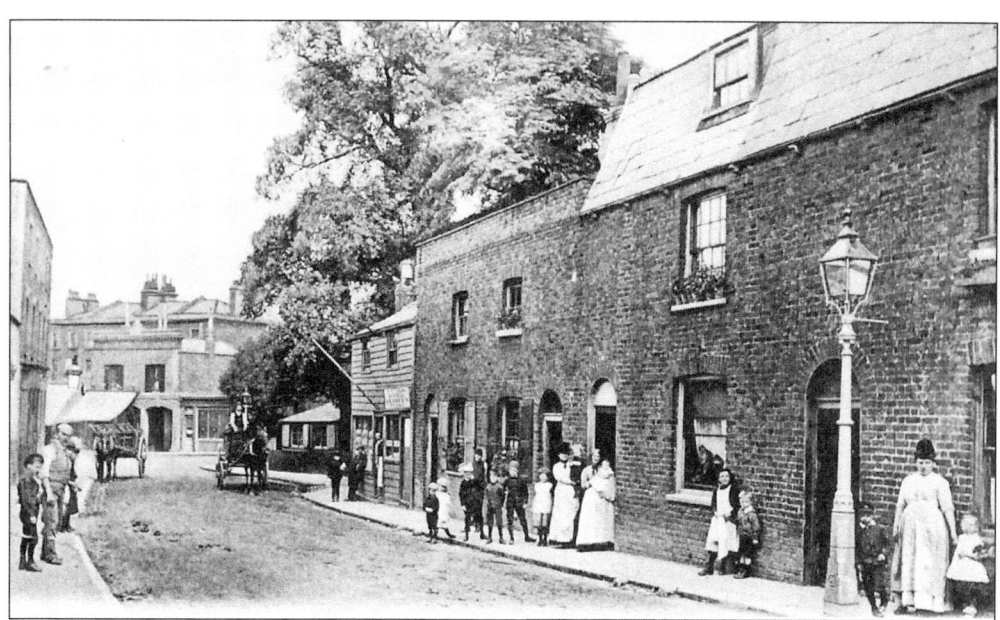

Above the smithy, on the east side of Crouch End Hill, were half a dozen brick cottages. Dating back to at least the 1860s, most survived until the 1930s. The gas street lamp is one of 120 installed by Hornsey in 1869. This view is dated 1890.

The Kings Head stood on the west side of Crouch End Hill, slightly higher up than when it was rebuilt in 1892. The records of the pub date back to 1662 and it would be a useful crossroads inn for travellers to and from London.

The Kings Head as rebuilt (right) on the corner of Coleridge Road (named in tribute to the poet who lived in Highgate). The Victorian pub provides lively entertainments in the 1990s. Left is Criterion Buildings with a crown decoration, possibly for Edward VII's 1902 coronation. Christ Church steeple can be seen.

Beyond the cottages on the east side of Crouch End Hill was this row of shops, seen here in 1890. Among services offered were shirt-making, harness-making, chimney-cleaning and picture-framing. The shops were swept away in 1938 when Mountview telephone exchange was established on the site. The Railway Tavern was rebuilt.

Higher up on Crouch End Hill were larger houses shielded by mature trees. One house on the corner of Haslemere Road was used by Charles Swinstead to found a private art school, later to develop into Hornsey School of Art, rebuilt in 1931. In 1984 it became the Trades Union Council Residential Education Centre.

Crescent Road, on the opposite (west) side of Crouch End Hill, was laid out by 1871 by Charles Scrase Dickens as part of his development of this area. It encircles Christ Church; nine of the substantial Gothic style mansions survive from the original development.

Coolhurst Road and Avenue Road, both leading out of Crescent Road, were among those laid out for C.S. Dickens who named it after the Regency house called Coolhurst near Horsham, Sussex, where he lived. Through the agency of the Imperial Property Investment Company, Dickens laid out some 121 acres derived from Rowledge Farm, a medieval church property, stretching towards Highgate.

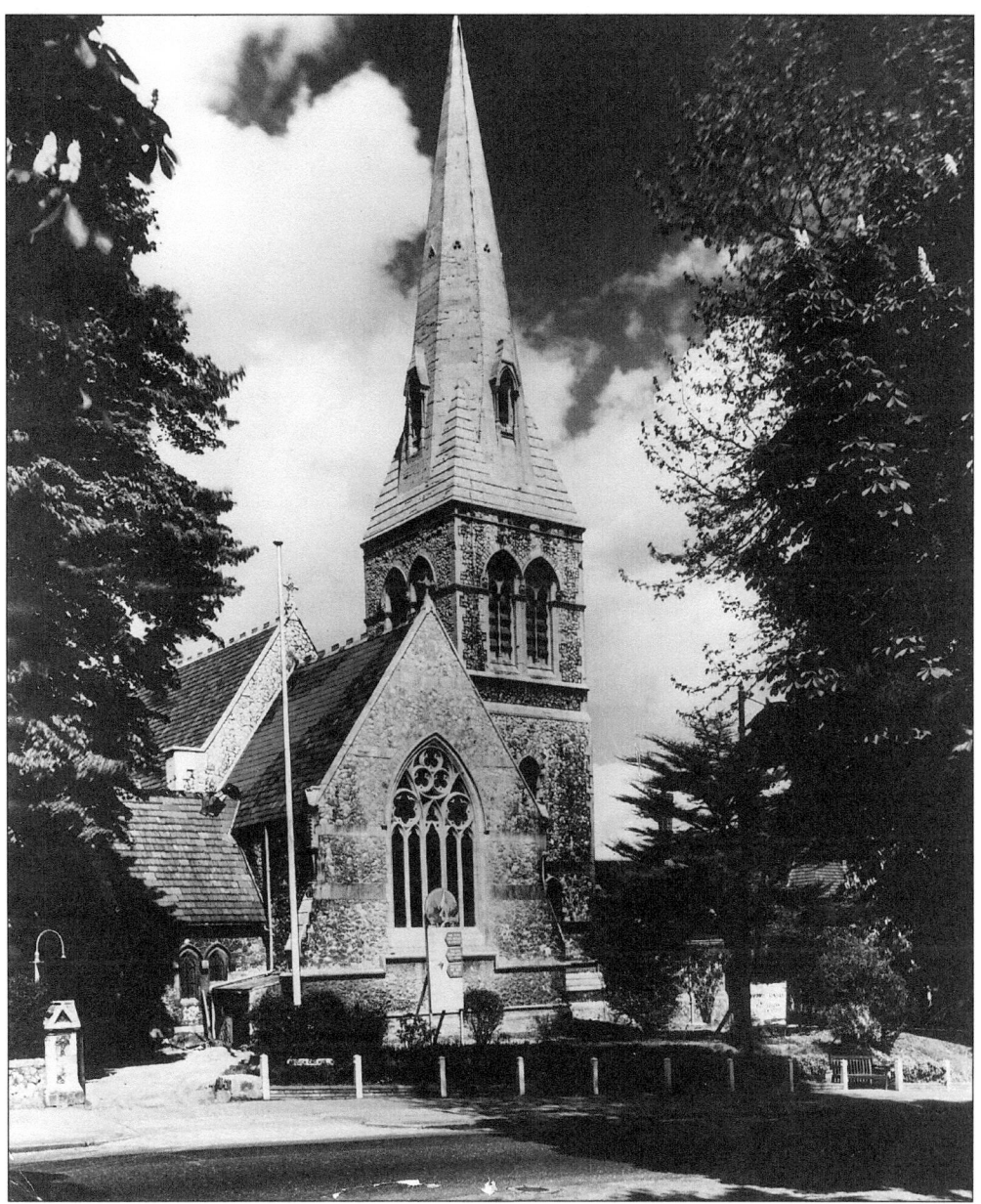

Christ Church was begun in 1861 as Crouch End's new parish church, replacing Broadway chapel. It was one of six churches to be created by Richard Harvey, Rector of Hornsey, during his tenure (1829-81). Possibly its name was chosen because of the religious reform movement centred around Christ Church college, Oxford, at that time. The site was given by C.S. Dickens. The architect was Arthur William Blomfield (1822-99), son of a Bishop of London, who was to design Holy Innocents' in Tottenham Lane in 1877. Constructed in Gothic style in grey Kent rag stone rather than brick, at the request of the Building Committee, it was extended in 1867 with a south aisle. In 1873 the tower and spire were added and in 1881 a porch. In 1906 architect W.A. Pite enlarged the north aisle and added other porches. The interiors were originally in coloured brick. Land lower down the hill was acquired to build Edison Hall, named like the road in which it stands, after the United States inventor.

Crouch End railway station stood at the top (eastern) side of the hill opposite a large house called The Limes and the southern end of Crescent Road. It was opened in 1867 by the Great Northern Railway Company on a new branch line from Finsbury Park to Edgeware. Footpaths radiated from the station to nearby large houses; some of the pathways survive. The brick booking office led to a footbridge down to two platforms. Herbert Clarke's coal order office stood nearby.

Crouch End station's two platforms in 1910. Passenger services ceased in 1954 and freight services in 1964. By the end of 1971 the track had been taken up and the line had become part of the Parkland Walk. The station was demolished and the bridge remodelled with a parapet of inverted arches.

Crouch End Hill leads into Hornsey Rise and Hornsey Road, both in Islington. Hornsey Lane runs south west from the top of Crouch End Hill towards Highgate, along the parish boundary between Islington and Hornsey. In the 1860s the Hornsey side of Hornsey Lane was still farmland. After Crouch End station opened in 1867 some twenty-one detached houses were built on its north side.

The entrances to Nos 62 and 64 Hornsey Lane. Hats were worn in Victorian times even by the gardener using a besom broom to sweep a drive. Servants were in all large houses and in smaller homes as well.

Hornsey Lane in 1890 with Hornsey on the left and Islington on the right. The gentleman is riding an Otto Dicycle, a form of tricycle invented in 1879. Tricycles enjoyed a vogue in the 1880s and 1890s and were considered more suitable for riders of shorter stature than the penny farthing bicycle.

The scene in Hornsey Lane above is still recognizable a century later, but the big houses on the Islington side have been replaced by blocks of flats. Some of the older houses survive on the Hornsey side.

Hornsey Lane in 1905 with a group of four watching the photographer. Behind them is Trays Hill Hall estate, an important Islington property dating back at least to the seventeenth century. In 1911 the occupant was a doctor. The road slopes downhill towards Crouch End Hill with Hazleville Road on the right. This lane is reputed to be an ancient route, possibly a prehistoric ridgeway.

Hornsey Lane, on a ridge leading towards Highgate, was in the path of a proposed bypass road devised to avoid steep Highgate Hill. In 1812 the new road was begun but the tunnel intended to drive under the ridge collapsed. A cutting was made instead, with Hornsey Lane carried over it by a stone archway, designed by John Nash, which was to give its name to Archway Road.

Traffic on Archway Road increased, with tolls abolished in 1876, and the stone arch was seen as too narrow. An iron bridge to carry Hornsey Lane was opened in 1900, allowing electric trams to run along Achway Road from 1905. In the 1960s the Islington section of Archway Road (south of the bridge) was widened further.

Ten

Celebrations
and Events

Park Road Open Air Swimming Pool was opened in 1929 and proved very popular at a time when outdoor pursuits were becoming fashionable and lidos being built. In 1975 the indoor pools were added but the outdoor pool continues to be opened in the summer to meet heavy demand.

The band of the local Territorial Army leads a detachment down Nightingale Lane towards Priory Road. The Drill Hall is to be seen on the right. The parade is part of the 1935 Jubilee celebrations to mark George V's twenty-five years on the throne.

A Territorial Army detachment marches along Priory Road past Nightingale Lane to its adjacent Drill Hall. This is part if Hornsey's parade to mark the Silver Jubilee of George V.

Territorial Army soldiers assemble for the 1935 Jubilee Parade outside their Drill Hall, built in 1900 on the site of Elm House in Priory Road. The earlier Volunteer Battalions were made part of the Territorial Army when it was created in 1908. The 7th Battalion, based here, was the first Territorial Army battalion to go overseas when they went to Gibraltar in 1915, then into fierce fighting on the Western Front in France. Names of those who died are on the War Memorial at Hornsey Central Hospital in Park Road. The Drill Hall has subsequently been rebuilt.

Priory Park, where the Silver Jubilee celebrations to mark the 25 years on the throne of George V are well under way.

The 1935 Silver Jubilee celebrations and the Major of Hornsey holds aloft a young girl who possibly has won a competition. The mayor at the time was Alderman William Grimshaw, who was later knighted. In 1955 his name was given to a secondary modern school in Creighton Avenue, Muswell Hill, later merged into Creighton school and subsequently renamed Fortismere School.

Unemployment and depression followed the 1929 Wall Street crash and the Borough of Hornsey sought the creation of local jobs. 'Answer the Mayor's Appeal and spend to create Employment' read the placards as the mayor assembles a team of supporters in period costume at the foot of the Clock Tower. The Mayor of Hornsey 1929-31 was Councillor C.H. Summersby MP.

A wheelbarrow race run on the North Middlesex Cricket Club grounds on Crouch End Playing Fields. W.G. Grace is among the cricketers who have played there.

The coronation of George VI on 12 May 1937 was marked throughout the country by celebrations. Hornsey had its carnival parade with decorated floats. Woolworths used its float to advertise Outdoor Girl beauty products, with suitably attired ladies emphasizing the outdoor theme.

W. Ham & Sons, fishmongers and poulterers, of 14 High Street, N8, entered this decorated delivery bicycle in the Borough of Hornsey Coronation Carnival procession of 1937. The firm had been at their shop in the High Street near Birkbeck Road for at least twenty-five years. Local wet fishmongers were always popular, especially in the days when they delivered. Supermarkets have severely reduced their numbers in recent years. George VI was George V's second son; the eldest assumed the throne as Edward VIII in January 1936 but abdicated in December 1936.

Opposite: A United Dairies milk float takes part in the 1937 Coronation Carnival procession. Horses continued to be used by milk distributors as well as coal merchants and others well into the 1960s.

This 1937 Coronation Carnival float carries a telvision transmission mast in imitation of the one erected at Alexandra Palace for the world's first public television service in 1936. The Hospital Savings Association running the float argue that you can afford three pennies a week for good sound and vision, even if you could not afford television.

Pupils at Crouch End High School and College probably enjoyed the Coronation Carnival. This 1929 photograph shows them at Elm House in Middle Lane where the school had been since 1914. The founder was the notable Charlotte Cowdray (1864-1932) in the centre, wearing spectacles. The school moved to Hornsey Lane in 1936 and closed in 1973.

Priory Park, again the location for festivities, this time for the 1937 coronation celebrations. Was this a competition for the best child and dog?

Decorated houses and street parties were the usual thing before modern motorized traffic made them difficult to arrange. This is the scene in Hornsey Road when the 1937 coronation celebrations were taking place.

The British Legion float for the 1937 Coronation Carnival seems to be an Army vehicle. Men and women in uniforms of all kinds sit upon it.

Christmas dinner in 1938 held by the British Legion in their Crouch End headquarters in Elder Avenue. Standing by the Push Bar door is Mr Strawson, who had a shop in Park Road. The young men and women present would in less than a year witness the outbreak of war and doubtless be swept up into it.

Opposite: The roller skating rink at Alexandra Palace was popular for decades. The north west of the building attracted people from afar. Kept open during the Second World War, it had to be closed in 1974 because of a dangerous roof. When rebuilt after the 1980 fire it was decided, in the time of high popularity for Torvill and Dean, to have ice skating there.

St Mary's church, Hornsey, and the last Remembrance Day service held under the auspices of the Borough of Hornsey. Soon the church itself would go. Considered unsafe, it was demolished under the St Mary (Hornsey) Act 1969.

British Legion, Hornsey Branch banners are held aloft at the 1964 Remembrance Day service. Since the demolition of St Mary's, services are held in the Garden of Remembrance at the foot of the medieval tower in Hornsey churchyard.

Hornsey was to disappear as a local authority in 1965 when the London Borough of Haringey took over the Borough of Hornsey and the Boroughs of Wood Green and Tottenham. One of the last Hornsey ceremonies took place on 10 December 1964 in Hornsey Town Hall, Crouch End. Town Clerk W.B. Murgatroyd (left) watches Alderman G.F. Norman sign, while Mayor Lawrence Bains stands to the right. To the rear are Alderman H. Williams and Alderman Peter Rigby. The Borough of Hornsey, formed in 1903, had been governed by a mayor, twelve aldermen (elected for six years) and thirty-six councillors (elected for three years).

Hornsey Borough Arms were granted in 1904. Oak trees symbolize its previously forested state and the crossed swords its connection with the See of London. The motto translates as 'The stronger because the more prepared'.

Crouch End Broadway is for many the heart of the district and, with the town hall, had once been the Borough's civic centre. In this 1930s view it is United Dairies on the corner of Weston Park in place of the creamery run by H. Williams. Other shops now gone, such as Tip Top and Burton the Tailor, can be seen. Traffic signals are in place but the quantity of traffic will in the 1990s fill the streets. Yet it retains a village feel.

Index